Ceremonies for No Repair

Ceremonies for No Repair

Paula Cisewski

Beauty School Editions, LLC

2024

First Edition

Cover art ("Ghost of Human Contact #4"), design, layout, and interior artwork: Paula Cisewski

ISBN 13: 979-8-9890962-1-3
www.beautyschooleditions.com

Minneapolis / White Bear Lake

To my son.

To everyone who survived the time of the pandemic.

To everyone who did not.

To my mother.

TABLE OF CONTENTS

Courage (n.)

c. 1300 corage, "heart" (as the seat of emotions.... Meaning "Valor, quality of mind which enables one to meet danger and trouble without fear."

www.etymonline.com

A red thread
A dead thread.
A tangle at the
inner part of who
mistook
extinction
for amnesia?
No. Opposite.
Am I discouraged
these coeur
words are not
bowtied to
care?

A RIVER CAN THE WAY A BODY CAN

Here by the riverbank everything's
frozen—bare branches balance vacated
nests—a squirrel leaps and bellydusts
the ruts of cross-country trails—

In summer I took sorrow here
to the river—dead marriage, dying
mother—it was uncontainable
not unlike big farm runoff or

our dumb-down guns or conceal
and carry TikTok accounts—I saw
a red fox here once but not today—
mostly clouds mostly other white

people with all the right gear
shooshing through the snow grooves—
in summer it was mostly vaccinated
people jogging too close to unvaccinated

people or vice versa—my private sorrow
lugged along and tossed in—the river
said yes—yes, I asked first—Hey
I don't want your sorrow gushing

downstream to my house said someone
but emotions are organic—a river
can thrash this one against a rock
dizzy it in eddies and transform any feeling

—I really must believe this—the way a body can
transform when a body can—last spring
my body could alter nothing and so I asked
the river—yes, I believed in it—

Hard to imagine in this later season
personal sorrow ever having trumped
any collective grief—when I say imagine

I mean remember—imagine spring—a river—

a thaw that mirrors a healing—a bald eagle
migration—all the returned kinds of green—
hard to remember how sorrow governed
last summer and hard to imagine

whether the bottom feeders of the Mississippi—
below the current sheets of ice—gulped up
then spat into the silt when—along with my sorrow—
I tossed over the bridge—my wedding ring

April 1, 2020

Today was the day my online therapist could not stop herself from explaining *The Tiger King* to me for I'd guess five minutes. This viral Netflix show but I don't have Netflix.

In a notebook next to my laptop on the dining room table, I wrote her phrase, "They stuff the snakes full of drugs," right above the therapeutic homework she gave me: Savor something every day.

It's funny. Ha-ha funny or peculiar funny: can't tell. It's funny. I'm not laughing. My therapist's hands are full of big gestures, unguarded, and more animated than I've seen in our two months together.

It's funny I'm not laughing, except a forced little to be polite. Why.

Surprise cry in the session's final minutes.

I despise crying in front of anybody, even a professional, even online, even just the Zoom box of my suddenly crumpled face.

Then our session was over; my online therapist's re-guarded, well-coiffed blonde head disappeared from my screen. Black square there. I closed my laptop, descended to the basement, and bagged up a seventh load of the garbage my husband left behind when he left me suddenly, two months ago.

My husband left me. I am sick*. It's nearing the second official month of sheltering-in-place in the U.S.

It is unlike me to say how I am with such candor, but I think I am unlike myself now, perhaps permanently.

*I do not (only) mean I am sick with the grief of a surprise divorce: This April Fool's is Day 24 of self-quarantine, which began with illness a week before the rest of the State of Emergency lockdown.

There aren't Covid-19 tests. Yet. An Urgent Care visit swab up my nose provided negative results for influenza A and B. I was often bedridden with a spiking fever, a headache, a punishing cough, exhaustion. Applying eucalyptus oil one night, I noted nothing, no smell, the lost sense. Later, conjunctivitis, ear infection. At a second Urgent Care visit my fever was low but my blood pressure and pulse were high.

I'm mostly well, if still easily out of breath, and it was sunny when it wasn't supposed to be.

Outdoors, I frittered the afternoon away in the bare garden. Frost in the shadows. Brown grass. Last year's dead weeds.

A red-tailed hawk coasted by.

GHOST OF HUMAN CONTACT

Stationed across a quarantine, one solitary night after another.
Light years between each star, to our eyes a constellation implies a whole.

One friend said as the group planned our next Zoom meeting,
"My asshole calendar still asks for the location of events."

After months of sheltering, I wrote cold mirages. I had no idea outside of winter.

Every room of the house a kind of altar I roamed through. Votives on the sills: lit overtures.

"See" you soon, we text each other. Yes scare quotes. Smiley face emoji. Heart.

Heart heart. All year I will want to be more, more what, but often I'll just sulk away polar vortex nights in front of HBO Max in a new relationship with my own resistance, developing a twitch in my upper lip. The whole world a single-minded wish I hadn't previously thought to notice.

To be more everything. Remember possible desire, falling ringless. Remember:
two separate, equally stupid dreams about romantic longing. Grief and grief and grief, then dinner.

Early on it was suggested we hug a tree. We were told: know you're not alone in feeling alone.

Loud music as rice boils. Big Joanie in the kitchen. Dance away the invisible feelings.

In the dreams I was either searching for something or hiding from something. Unclear. Like waking life, it could have been a both/and situation.

In winter, a body waits—like any seed in a pouch—equal measure neither resurrection nor burial: plumule of a future encased in a shell.

SECRETS THE DANDELIONS KNEW

As they came bursting through the snow in my dream:

I wasn't afraid, though they burst forth rapidly, tall
as me, taller. I let them giant, wanting to see what

would happen: the taproots feeding off his love rot,

yellowheads shouldering the cold out,
the mess out, anything not medicine

out. The way he was leaving me

I didn't know I knew. A dream blooming,
in which I knew and wasn't afraid. I was

thirsty for bitters, for the earth

to swallow whole what choked me.
I wasn't worried whether he'd like the wild

garden* no one asked for. I liked it.

I was amazed: out of scale in a state
of wonder, which wants me ever faithful.

---

*I dreamed the dandelions months ago, before Gone Husband was physically gone, but while he had become an unknowable man who did not love me. I dreamed the dandelions shortly before or after he said *You're always mad now* then fell asleep in his chair while I tried responding. The sound of my voice a shut-down drug. I dreamed the dandelions before or after I asked

---

where he went at night and he said *G5 might cause mass extinction we don't know*. Before he said *You never believed in me.*

Before I said *Your behavior is manic**; I'm afraid*.
Before he said *Oh so I'm crazy?*
Before he said *Oh so I'm psychotic?*

April Something, 2020

Today was the day my mother called. I answered while clearing the eighth or fifteenth bag of husband trash from the basement. Her hip replacement surgery has been postponed indefinitely. There are no hospital beds. Years she's hurt. Years she's wanted her doctor to prescribe her "the good pain pills," but he won't. She'll become an addict she thinks he thinks. She's nearly 83.

She tells me that my dad, 86, is still going out mid-pandemic to the grocery store, "because it's the only place that has my good, gluten-free bread." I scolded a little. Offered to pay for their deliveries, which they don't need me to do (scold or pay).

A dreary, rainy, slow day. A little too like a mirror.

**Why did I use the word *manic*. Stupid. Stupid. *I'm not angry* I said then, always angry, always shamed by anger. What was happening any given day? Body had become like a mad board, vigilant with confused fury-terror. Husking such grief. As a wife I was a felled tree.

IS THIS VICTORY?

—*after* Winged Victory of Samothrace *and a postcard by Alec Soth*

It feels like whoever lives
here never moved in. Like
a bare bulb switched on in a vacant
back room. Like a portrait of a stranger

hung on an otherwise blank
box of walls.   We all live
some days like a body with no
head and others like a head with

no body. Where do our missing
halves hide? We can text them
and hope for a selfie sent
back from Wherever, looking

just like an angel, or, I suppose,
like what's left of one.

An alert pings at 2am: First thought: Is my son okay? The bots had just compiled an album titled "Together." Thumbnail images: Gone Husband's and my tiny happy heads leaning in toward each other in front of a waterfall, Gone Husband's and my tiny happy heads leaning in toward each other in front of a Ferris wheel. I had just nodded off, having stayed awake too long interacting with double screens: the TV screen for pandemic news and the tablet screen for no-sew face mask patterns. I crawled back under the blankets and deleted the two photos, then photo after photo, like uncounting sheep.

UNBECKONING GLASS: A MEMORY

This color is exhaled smoke from a bummed cigarette, a stray cloud for the sky.
The color of adjoining rooms and is the door chained on the other side.

Outside the two soaked bars of this color, a lighter gray lives, like the invisible
sun wants to peek through all the marginalia of love.

Two people are having a talk they already had in this color.
A lot of pauses around the rain which erupts in this color.

And time builds its promise towers in the fog of this color.
Revoked words live inside the eraser smudge of this color.

This color is dusk. Many people feel unsettled by dusk.
Give us day or night; I can’t be inside my own skin

in the gloaming when our shadow selves get all their big ideas.
The gaze of this color is a soft equal sign. Two twin beds childish or sexless as graves.

The conversation performed in this color harkens back to what’s unlovable.
The performance of the original wound as general malaise.

This color wants to touch itself or is that the other?
Either way there's no touching in this color except by this color.

Two people are still having a talk they already had in this color.
What kind of color protects possibilities from coming into focus

by bending light into mirages. Mirages are the thirst and TV
snow of this color, and the apartment walls you'll lose your security

deposit if you paint. This color has the acoustics of packing
paper, a ghost's idea of home. This color is the God of Double

Negatives. The God of Stiff Equivalence. The God
of Blowing Dust Bunnies out from Under our Beds.

April 4, 2020

And yet, don't I savor something every day?

I opened my campus email to find a former student wrote just to say she still does the "tiny pleasures" prompt I assign around midterm and finals weeks, when stress peaks for most.

It's not a gratitude list. It's just this: list any small thing that makes your days a little nice. As an example, I had told her class: it's pleasing when I'm filling a bottle in a public fountain with a display that counts plastic bottles saved and the number goes up one. It won't make it into my memoir, but it's nice.

The last time I filled a bottle in public was almost a month ago.

My former student wrote that she is always pleased by the way country singers pronounce the month "July." Jooo-lyyyh.

When I read that this practice is helping her shelter in place, a tiny surprise cry. I thanked her.

This sweet gesture from a person I will likely never see again.

It's raining. I had just watered my plants: pothos, snake plant, hibiscus, Norfolk pine, hoya carnosa compacta, philodendron, monstera, jade. I wrote back that it pleases me to water my houseplants on rainy days, so they don't feel left out.

April 5, 2020

1,200 deaths in the US in the last 24 hours.

Over 10 million people in the US are newly unemployed.

What is the purpose of keeping my one self alive?

Even a dandelion is useful. Makes pollen, is one hundred percent medicinal. Is cheerful early on when people and other creatures are starved for color. Frustrates lovers of too much structure. If I am going to continue, can I be more like a weed?

Every day in the spring garden is the day a red-tail hawk coasts by, but today there were two making slow spirals. A hawk helix.

The Tennessee Department of Health "advises health care workers to use swim goggles as eye protection; plastic bags as gloves; and tissue, gauze, and diapers as masks."

April 7, 2020

Strange dreams about my mom. At one point she was running, just running, for pleasure, an activity she has never once done and would not have been physically able to do for the last many decades.

I could feel the joy on my mother's dreamface throughout my body. As if hers were my body. As if I were her.

Mother was running through a lush green field of wildflowers: dandelions, daisies, lady slippers, brown-eyed Susans. I could feel the breeze on her skin as if it were my skin. As if I were her. Was she young? She was a child, and she was my mother.

There are so many protections up and around the way I am able to give to and receive love in this relationship.

I rarely dream of her.

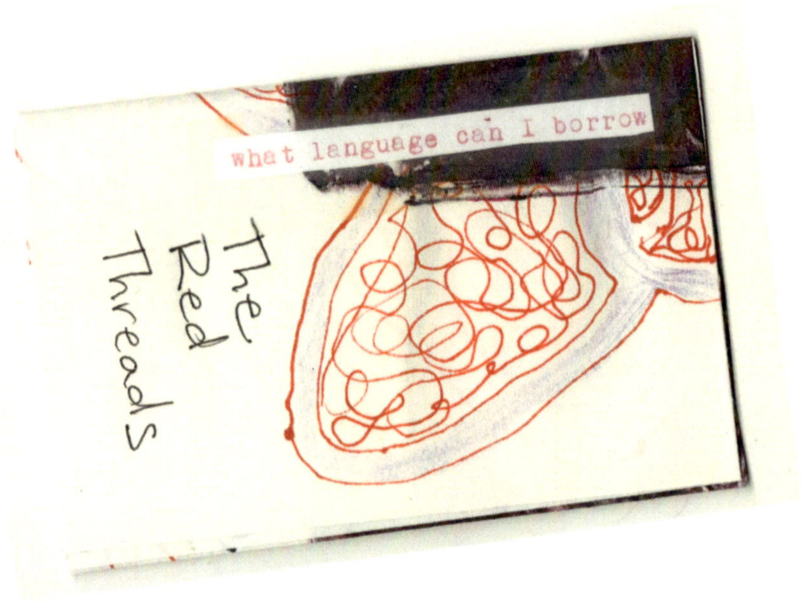

April 14, 2020

1.9 million confirmed cases and 120,000 global deaths from the virus, *Democracy Now!* reports.

April 17, 2020

In the evening, in the bedroom, I moved some of my own clothes into my grandmother's dresser, which has been sitting empty, which for eleven years held Gone Husband's things.

I dripped some clary sage oil into a diffuser and placed it on the bed stand that used to be his, along with a candle and some flat stones from the shore of Lake Superior. I considered that half of the bed, that vacancy I've been sleeping next to for more than two months.

I spread my whole body across the whole mattress.

Rituals to make this space feel wholly mine, not half empty.

April 20, 2020

Today is the day my mother describes her hallucinations to me from the hospital: Red strings everywhere.

No one can visit.

When my dad brought her to the ER last night, he had to wait alone in his car for two hours holding his cell phone for news. It had dipped to freezing temperatures again. He's 86.

She is suddenly suffering from a condition none of us has ever heard of* caused by a serious underlying condition none of us was aware of.

Hearing her describe her hallucinations today—amused by the little person, like an angel elf she says, looking at her from on top of the dresser—is better than hearing her last night living inside her hallucinations in confused fear.

She sees red strings on everything.

---

*

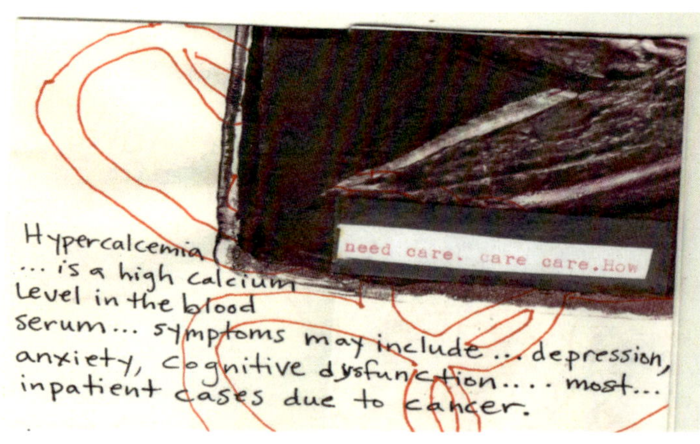

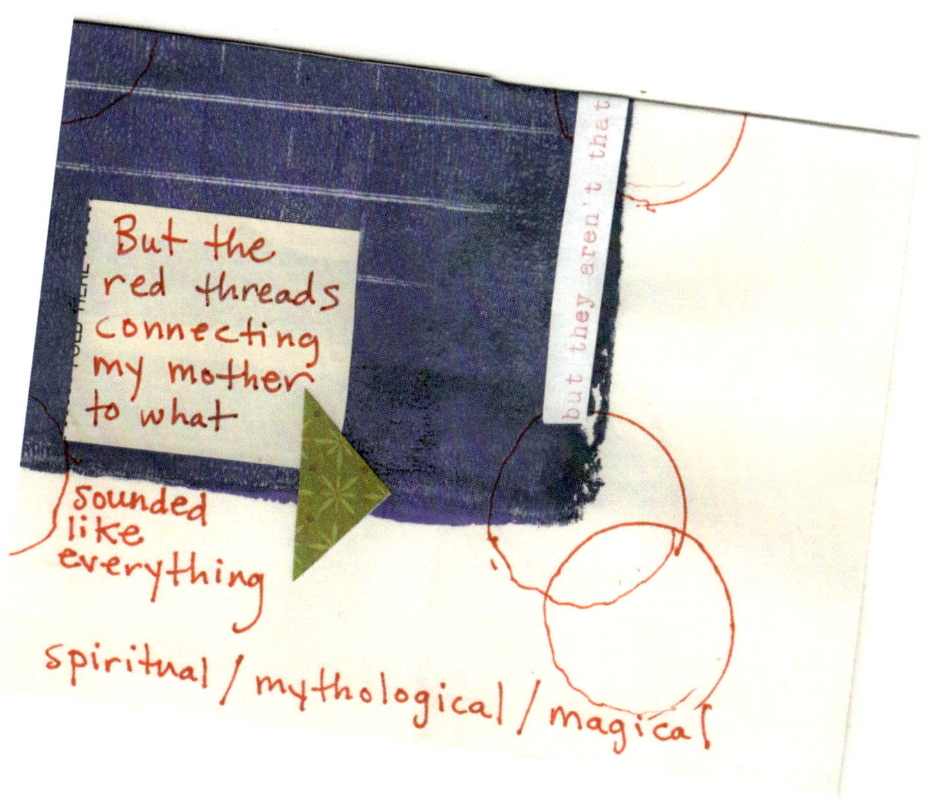

April 24, 2020

Today The President of The United States of America suggested injecting disinfectants to cure Covid-19.

April 26 or 27, 2020

Dug up so many hostas from around the yard and wheeled them out to a friend to load up in her van. Physical exhaustion as a substitute for physical contact.

Over 40,000 confirmed Covid-19 deaths in the US.

I knew dandelions were magic. The bitterness of dandelions cleanses organs. The leaves are diuretic.

But I didn't know how else they are magic. I learn in an online workshop on menstruums and tinctures that dandelion helps us heal ancestral trauma.* That they help us connect with our ancestors. That they help us recognize physical needs.

What is my ancestral trauma? What are my physical needs?

Today we find out what kind of cancer mom has, and how progressed.

---

*Mom says, *Do ya know what I do about the red strings? I imagine a dustbuster in my hand, and I vacuum them all up!*

Here is my mother's mother, and here she is, too. Two sisters. Mabel, on the right, we never knew, having died from complications of childbirth one day after delivering my mother. Doris, on the left, we knew. And loved. My clothes are in the dresser inhereted from her. She and her husband Howard raised my mother. The family kept the adoption a secret, or they tried to.

May 1, 2020

How any one body can house so much simultaneous gratitude and ugly. I woke today, a woman-shaped war zone. Happy May Day.

After he left, it took me three weeks to share the news with my parents, and then I shared it chickenshit by email.

Two breakups and almost two decades earlier, I shared the news of a different ending. My mother, giving her best effort toward maternal instinct, said, "Ohhhhh, why do they always leave you?" Which they didn't.

Picked dandelions and dried nettles for myself and for friends. For the deep green trace minerals, for the healing sting.

That mother ohhhhh held for three syllables at least.

May 10, 2020

It's Mother's Day. Someone didn't love you right. Who cares.

Have I ever been so in-between for so long? Such a dandelion seed on the wind?

My son comes by with soup, vitamins, candy. He sits on the porch and I sit inside and we visit through my picture window.

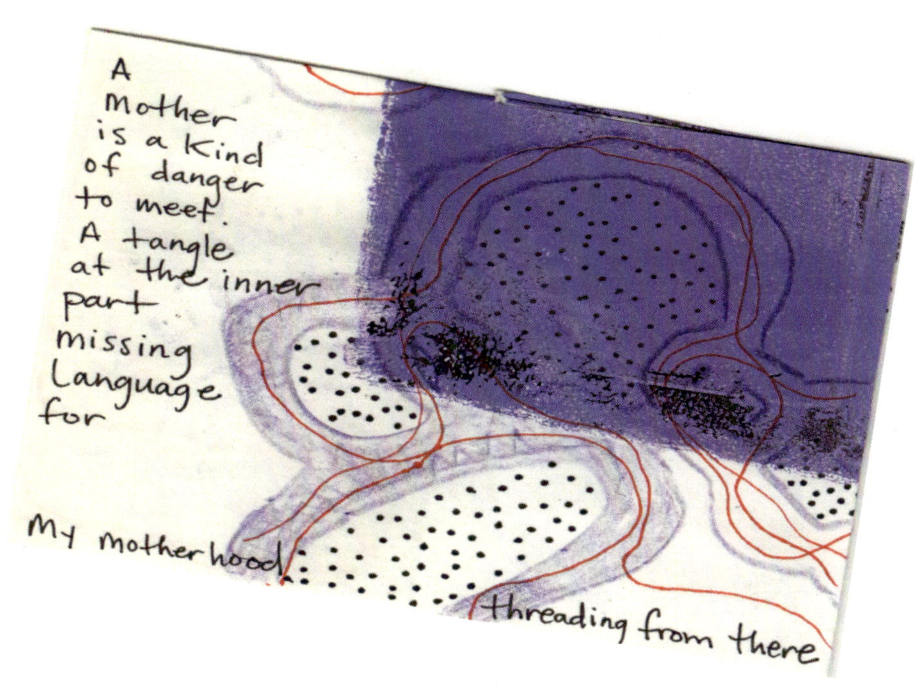

After the adoption, my mother's birth father became her uncle and raised her older siblings as her cousins. Sometimes they lived on the same small town street.

May 15, 2020

Democracy Now! runs a clip of the actual President of The United States of America saying, "If we didn't do any testing, we would have very few cases."

May 22, 2020

On the table: a bud vase spilling fragrant tiny white lilies of the valley. Two vases jammed full of lilacs, dogwood blossoms, and bleeding hearts. Either things will get better or I will die in a beautifully blooming terrible time.

Next to the bouquets, my virtual therapist's face on a laptop screen. She says, *Who says you have to forgive anyone?*

May 24, 2020

343,000 Covid-19 deaths globally.

MOTHER CORONA

1.
A name is a plucked bloom that outlives you.
Hers: Arlene. Mother. Other. Never

forgotten exactly, never secret,
not resting, unsaid through the hurt hours while

her cancer's thriving, even as racists
and a virus swarm. The world uncouples

itself screen-by-screen, then redoubles pod-
by-pod our bubbles. I overmother,

underdaughter, troubling myself, my loved
ones, asynchronously. Losses garland

the budding solitudes. One's universe:
some hollow stem, some scatter-seed names.

Can I chain together the looped wishes, like
that thing kids chant over dandelions.

May 28, 2020

Morning online Interfaith vigil for George Floyd.

South Minneapolis burned last night. Police on roof-tops shot rubber bullets into peaceful crowds, tear gassed seated teenagers in the street.

Mom was in another realm, uninterested in whatever a telephone is today. I felt a tether slackening.

MOTHER CORONA

2.
That thing kids chant over dandelions
is MOMMA had a BABY and her HEAD
POPPED OFF! Which head? Which her?

Or some kid would put a fat bloom beneath
your chin and if the flesh glowed yellow, you
liked butter. Do you like butter? Do you

hate mother? Must you weave a flower crown
of other? To purge the bitterness of
the mutter? Oh Ma, Momma, Mother, no

expensive bouquet delivered to your
bedside will brighten with cheery yellow
and ribbon these hours we don't call your last.

Our Long-Suffering Mother in Quarantine
is not the first line of anything bright.

Mother's birth father, Casimir Boho, was born in Poland. Once, I was a teenager who didn't understand our lineage and I asked if she was Polish, too. *I ain't no Polack!* she growled a real growl at me, her Polish daughter and in front of her 100% Polish husband. A denial continued, cutting threads.

GHOST OF HUMAN CONTACT

What is memory. So many photos
document peak moments from stories that
slope low later. Time will give every story
an ending. What are endings. I'm in the basement

clearing out the ex's trash. How's this guitar still here.
Pearl acoustic buried behind married years. It was mine once
but I recall giving it away. I could only ever play
Sinead O'Connor's "Black Boys on Mopeds"

which uses the same chords as Neil Young's "Helpless" and
probably a lot of other songs, too. You think you're
playing one song and someone tells you you're playing
another. After the last bag went in the can, I didn't know

what to do with the hollow sadness, so I drove to Home
Depot and sat there in the lot, radio off, nebulously wanting,
no shopping list. I watched the slow parade of people push
carts, trying with vinyl flooring or leaf blowers to make their

homes better homes. Just because you're right doesn't mean
another person's not also right, but goddamn it. I know
which song I used to play, and it wasn't "Helpless."
It's not that time gives stories endings, what does

any begun thing do but end; it's the new understanding
of some particular endings. What is understanding.

MOTHER CORONA

3.
Is not the first line of anything bright
a lighter held to a past's fuse? The past,

more flammable than imaginable, so
I'll forge ahead in this poem with all the Ohs.

Enough enough. Mother never was a good
audience for the offerings of her budding

jokesters, oh no, laughter prompted rage a bough
breaking: Jesus, nobody's making fun

of you. Oh Mom, Oh Ma, I know you loved
your children and never quite understood

happiness. My sudden unhelpful impulse
in your last days to call out Momma, Mom-

ma to the familiar want of you, though
here you are not. Oh. The mother we knew.

AS IF WONDER WERE THE ILLNESS

We had entered into a dark time.
The advice on repeat was Trust

the grieving process, but we'd already
thrown trust a disappointing funeral. Sparse

mourners. Sad luncheon ham.
Then the refrain changed to Hey,

at least we're still alive, which
is only ever true for some of us.

We put our masks on. We put
our other masks on. Now

we're hearing Pleasure is a construct not
a natural phenomenon. We hunker

down. Now we hear nothing.
Is this still the dirty clothesline we call

the dark time? When will the dark
time end? No word. Has it ended?

No one peeks through the curtains.
No one splits open the drawn blinds.

MOTHER CORONA

4.
Here you are not. Oh. The mother we knew
willed toward what belonging? Belonging
to time--all different times—strung together
between present versions of memories.

This voice of a sick person no one can see.
That young girl, that damaged Little Arlene.
Much of childhood is a convenient us,
a cub pack momentarily sans mommas.

Neighbor kids chanted their bright loss practice.
Some decades fully grown and still I am not prepared
to cajole the trauma-girl in her into wanting dinner
from a computer screen [insert image

of quarantine in oncology wing]
Mother will not eat her butter. It's too.

ROUND

It's never not birds but try
to write a poem during
the news about the news
after the news it's never
after the news write
a poem during the recent
outrage cycle after which
nothing changed it's never
after except something
changed

                                        not what we expected
and not how we imagined which
was what?   All At Once and
                                                          with an apology from
                                                          the president? Good one.

Even in our quarantines
people are so relieved
when spring arrives
the slop we hardly
register because some
red wing blackbirds
perch above the walk and
suddenly in our minds
it's not news it's hopscotch
and suddenly in our minds
it's never not birds but try

May 29, 2020

Helicopters all the time.
8pm curfew in a quarantine.
The officer who murdered George Floyd arrested, finally.

White guys driving trucks with no license plates all over town. Infiltrating protests. Inciting. Stacks of bricks for brains.

Flash of last night's dream in which a womanbeing—not quite human, not quite solid—laid cool hands over my eyes and said "Oh honey. We will have to do something about these."

MOTHER CORONA

5.
Mother will not eat her butter it's too
fattening. I'm finally losing weight
after failing all my life, says she.

Let's change the subject. What other golden

thing did childhood bring? I remember
seven: sugar bubbles sip sip a clean sting

and POOF went all my inhibitions. Drunk
on a thimbleful of champagne at brother's
graduation dinner, why I wondered

was everyone giving me amazed looks?
Temporary hero to my older
siblings: I had buzzed up scolded mother.

Momma had a baby and her head popped off.
Much like memory: yellow bud that was

GHOST OF HUMAN CONTACT

Yellow iris buttery
Fluttery falls and
Flounces drunk
In a vase of city water

The outer world
Begins with lovers
Ends in loss
There is no beginning

There is no end
There is only the circle
Some flowers being seasonal
So few planes nowadays

That when one flies by while
I'm making a poem I think
Hey a plane and say it
Out loud surprising myself

Look at a tree
I'm a person
But also I'm an echo
A tool or a weapon

Weeks spent rehashing
A neglected message
If I wasn't listening
No one was listening

An iris probably did not dream
All winter underground
To be beautiful enough
For cutting

AMOR FATI

What's the way to otherness? Lead the way.
If love departs, what is its destination?

Is love off to *Planet And* where we all go
when we're done being one, being

separate from other ones? As I write,
helicopters hack up the sunset. The city's

new curfew kicks in. I can't
hear you, *Momma Momma*. Who

can't hear whom? And
whom? And whom?

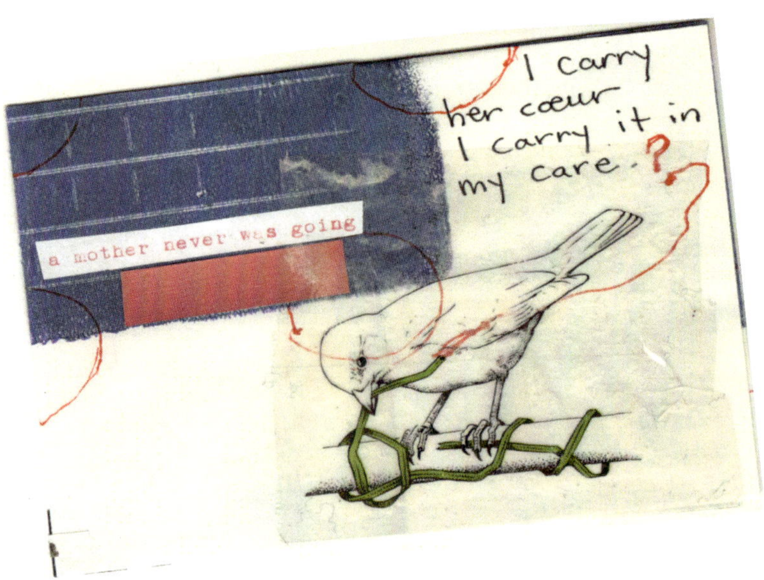

May 31, 2020

Does it matter what day of quarantine it is when the city has become a militarized zone? At yesterday's virtual artists' town hall I committed to doing what I can. (What can I?)

On a repeated news clip, a clutch of police walking down the middle of a Whittier neighborhood street firing rubber bullets at Black residents who were standing on their own porch.

Images of the demolished post office in the 5th precinct, whose mail service is suspended indefinitely.

Even with their go-bags packed, even between protests, even grieving, other artists were in that meeting, still organizing, still dreaming and working toward better.

I don't have much beyond small donations, but I have a spare room, so I offer it to some southside friends. They are afraid at home, yet we wonder how they would even get here. There's no route. Freeways barricaded. Downtown deeply militarized after a semi truck driver plowed through a crowd of protesters. No one killed, miraculously.

371,000 Covid-19 deaths globally.

Dry more nettles for care packages.
Work slowly on divorce forms for 30 awful minutes.

Hear Dad's plea when he calls: Do I think I can call and coax Mom into eating because she won't and can no longer stand.
I tried, but she didn't answer.

Sleep a little with many lights on, phone under my pillow, and the neighborhood WhatsApp thread bingbinging messages from frightened neighbors all night.

MOTHER

6.
Much like memory: yellow bud that was
Sometimes I like when a person's forgotten
Something I've said so I have the pleasure of
Saying it twice How is your garden
She asked already early in the call
The light fades I call my sister say Mom's
Dying tonight for sure when I cry
My adulthood fizzles still I want no
Consolation the light fades the world un-
Couples itself not every time not this time
In the morning I call the hospital
Again time proved me wrong our mother
Survived another night and quarantined
Suffering still, How is your garden she asks

CORONA

7.
Suffering still, How is your garden she asks
Again again here are lilacs, iris
The lavender yellow of a new spring
Dandelion dandelion she'd call them weeds
Pink roses red tiger lilies daisies
Appeared like goldenrod for bees milkweed for
Monarchs flit around the purple coneflower
Balm of anise hyssop, stinging nettle
Doing my best to tend abundance then
Like kudzu throttling the dogwood
Cabbage moths flutter hungrily and spurge
Cannot be saved everything cannot be
Saved or even tamed or even loved right
I don't know how anyone sleeps at night

MORNING PRAYER

Sunlight on the radishes and on
the beet shoots and on the hemlock
invading the plot. My shadow,

a sleepweeding blot, follows
along through the rhizosphere,
just above the underworld. Spider

in the trellis, shadow of a rose.
A pile of poison plants dying
above the dirt. I water

the rooted plants and drink
from the hose. Sunlight frizzles
my night head, where Chiron

moonwalks through the house
of my dad jokes. Dear Whichever
God: want is a stupid drug.

GHOST OF HUMAN CONTACT

You're someone I secretly love, and you're
also someone I secretly love, in such

a lonely springtime so much is growing
even as it doesn't know what's dying.

The accidental secret of the unsaid thing.

I love your face.
I love your face so much.

Even the hate-filled ones, someone's love can
deliver us from the hate-filled ones, Momma Momma, we

must deliver ourselves. Are you saying that or am I
saying that? Or is what's received eternally on repeat?

June 10, 2020

Two friends and I go masked to 38th and Chicago to visit the memorial that's evolved and evolving around the site of George Floyd's murder. I'm compelled to risk the crowd while believing and not believing I might be allowed to visit my mother any time soon.

Thousands of bouquets below murals, twelve-foot sculpture of a Black Power fist at the center of the intersection, the growing list of names of Black people murdered by police stenciled on the asphalt, music from a boom box, pop-up food shelves, bbq smoke, community, grief, hope, swirling enormity.

It's reverent, overwhelming. Everyone's masked, everyone is giving space to one another. We three each add to the existing offerings the small offerings we brought. From me, a small jade heart. An ever green.

MOTHER CORONA

8.
I don't know how anyone sleeps at night
I do not say to Mother whose terror
eyes fill an iPad screen or who receives
more fucking bouquets in her quarantine.

Where to place vases in a room she hates.
It's late May in her cancer. She'll never
hear of the uprising. Of the sprung up
encampments in city parks. No reason

to mention the squeal of bomb trains wheeling
fracked oil over rickety rail bridges
(I must shut the window to better hear her)
or the swelling bell of pandemic deaths.

No news, no appetite, no visitors, no hugs.
The flowers would be better if they were drugs.

June 18, 2020

Family video chat with Health Care Team. In one of five boxes on screen, a digital Mother and Not Mother, thinned and frightened in her bed, looking where. At the screen, at the little boxes of daughter, daughter, husband, then off again into the where. I too was staring at her face not the camera dot. No such thing as eye contact. Sister kept her face offscreen, having offscreen kinds of feelings. Father was doing his best stoicism. Nurse was looking at the camera so we feel like she looked at us as she delivered news, explained care plan.

GHOST OF HUMAN CONTACT

My garden is beautiful sometimes, not
just a ramshackle, necropastoral ode

to divorce in which a man-shaped sculpture
entitled Birds Wanted—charred scrapwood, rust

cockleburs—collapsed behind the house, its chest
a heart-shaped hole, no more for wren-nesting.

First lightning, then blizzard, then many
a natural vandal, including our

own entropy, arrived so willingly.
One worn arm dropped off, no big deal, into

the radish patch. Disarticulated,
it went with the rest to the scrap-heap.

Wild throttle-vine and violet, aphid and fear
a shoddy haven cleared. The birds still here.

MOTHER CORONA

9.
The flowers would be better if they were drugs
fucking up my dead pens   weed patches of pens
secretly haunted pens filled with ghost ink.
Whiling away   impotently at home   while
the white supremacists infiltrate this
city's uprising.   Hollow throat pens.   Lost
voice pens.   Do I idle   the entire
revolution at a kitchen table
not bringing Covid to my dying mother?
What I am afraid of now is not so
different from what I was afraid of back
when I believed I feared nothing.   I really said
I'm afraid of nothing. But I do fear
death documented in invisible ink.

MOTHER CORONA

10.
Death documented in invisible ink.
The daily calls go unbodied. Two voices:

It's Paula / I don't know / It's Paula your
daughter / Oh thank you. Can you turn the light

off? Can you turn the light off? / Not from here.
But I'm here. / Can you just turn everything

else off? Can you turn everything off?
Can you just turn the movie off? Can you

turn the movie off now? Turn off every
thing else? Can you just turn the nurse off?

Can you turn the nurse off now? / Not from here.
But I'm here. / Well, here we are then / Here we

are. / Yes. / A conversation in the weeds
A field of weeds and featherseeds in flight

WHAT IS BLUE IS MY MENTOR

—after a Wrecked Archive *photo*

I was talking to a friend—not in person
of course—on a screen from her new house,
alone, when a sudden shudder passed through her.

Did something just cross behind me? She asked.
I said I didn't see anything because dang it
I didn't see anything. Then it was bedtime.

I dreamed a new suitor had invented
ingestible music. A bowl of chewable songs
at a party. Each guest ate our favorite.

Enthralled by the feast of melodies, the strangeness
of dreaming up an entirely new person
when I haven't seen the old persons

in person in how-long-is-
quarantine didn't occur to me until
I woke in this world where again

a little vertigo reminds me I don't know
what I don't know, but there it hangs
on my screen, in my dreams, in the sky—

the sky which is thankfully brilliant if half haunted
as it canopies our dream bellies full of song—
the revised calendar and solitary event of the year.

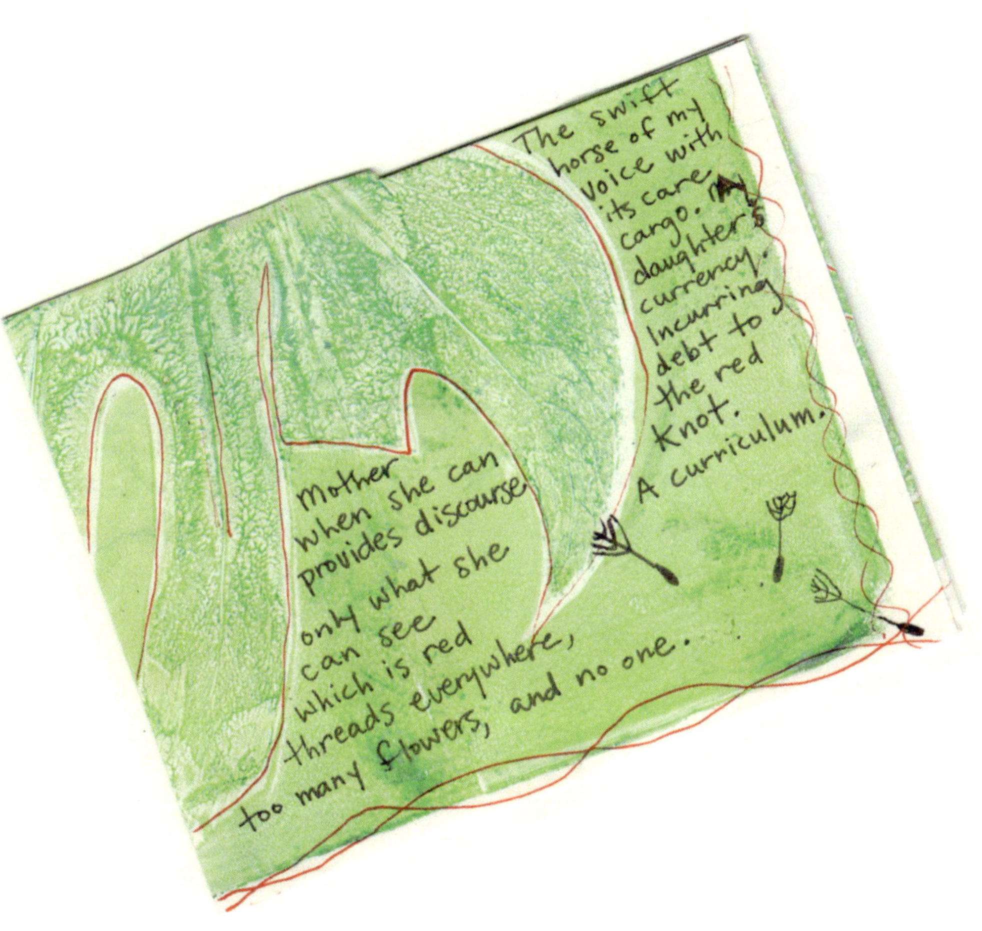

June 15, 2020

While I was working on the garden boxes, I received a text from my dad: *Call as soon as you can*, so I did, steeling myself for news I don't want.

Dad has a question about bread yeast. He has never called me with a question about bread yeast or any such domestic detail. It is not why he's calling now. He cries at the other end of the line. He cries in front of me for the first time in my life, and then he apologizes for it.

GHOST OF HUMAN CONTACT

Foolishly I think I am alone when   I'm alone when

here are my night people,   my dream flowers,

my epic nascent descent   through my indecent lexicon

of loss. As I cleared the years   of debris my husband left when

he left, from under his desk   two magnetic words surfaced: *bitter want.*

Here is my unwanting spell,   my sweetening, the bouquet

of thorns I bit the buds off.   Oh foolishly, how foolishly, I think

I'm alone when I'm accompanied   by every unapologetic letter

of the alphabet, up all night   and snoring through breakfast:

my chorus my clan my why.   Is the question I'm spelling out

How do I want the home I make or   How do I home the want I make?

Weekly I wake to the sound of my garbage being carried away, am texted an alert that my grocery delivery has arrived. Semi-monthly I have a therapy session on my computer screen with a woman I've never met in the real world. So many ways strangers—and money, as long as it lasts—are making a healing solitude possible. Am I healing?

MOTHER CORONA

11.
A field of weeds and featherseeds in flight:
Something's always bugging Little Arlene,
this time it's Little Brother who followed
her and Best Friend around after school, to

where they're reading funny pages under
an elm on a hill. She thinks the slur's "toe
head" and calls him that, tells him his head looks
just like a big toe and shakes her black curls.

She taunts him: "You're adopted. Adopted!"
But Best Friend knows a secret she's relieved
to release. Little Arlene's blond brother
is really her cousin. Her mom's her aunt.

Arlene learns she's the adopted one, like so.
Anyway, that's what messed up my mother.

MOTHER CORONA

12.
Anyway that's what messed up your mother
Mom says after describing her childhood
trauma scene in detail apropos of nothing
as I drove her to Great Granddaughter's flute
recital some years ago. You never
told me you were adopted, I said. Others
did. She said Oh. I didn't know you didn't
know. I was always talking about something.

Puritanical silences fueled rage.
Mother always wanted to be better.
Our walls jammed with motivational plaques
espousing the patience she lacked.

She's patient now, but Mother's got a little cough.
One more thing that seemed to come from nowhere

June 24, 2020

1,160,869 Global Covid-19 deaths

A friend and I were distance-visiting on my patio when the nurse called. Why was she calling me and not my father? In the ten minutes or so he was away from his phone, an emergency. Mom was being taken to the ICU with frighteningly low oxygen levels.

GHOST OF HUMAN CONTACT

Anyone can transform a solitude into the site of either failure or creation but don't forget to mute yourself or the host will do it for you.

I'm at the kitchen table in a virtual work meeting, and I'm on my phone again Googling what ex-wives do with the wedding gowns that ghost the backs of our closets. Some shred theirs, torch theirs, hem them short to wear on their revenge bods, or fly the gowns like kites. Some gowns get buried, funeral-style.

This screen that screen. My attention is often split between virtual spaces, which means I'm often more or less nowhere.

Locatable answers do not satisfy. The meeting ends. The Googling ends.

I walk through the park, notice two people: she's texting on a bench while he flies his drone over the baseball field. Imagine composing a eulogy for a gown; when my mother dies she'll be given no funeral. It's a pandemic.

So little traffic these days that city workers have cordoned off every other street for walkers so that when we emerge from our homes alone we can walk to the park alone, cross the center line alone.

I could give the gown to a child for dress-up, but I need never to glimpse it through a child's imagination.

Not to keep circling back to it, but yes actually, to keep circling back to it, what even is modern love? After months of fretting over lack of ritual, I return from a walk and throw the gown in the bin by the alley. Let it join the other trash in the dump where memories can't go.

Generally, I want to repurpose everything, but I cannot repurpose this gown. Not as kindling, as toy, as glamor, as charity, as corpse. Red gown reused only in language, which, like grief, and trash, is everyone's.

MOTHER CORONA

13.
One more thing that seemed to come from nowhere.
Mother's little cough is Covid. Even

in her lucid moments there was no mention
of goodbye. Unless that's what she meant when

she repeated I want to come home now
between small talk and hallucinations.

There's no more reconciling anything,
just a final day when we gather round

her hospital bed, finally allowed two
at a time in yellow jackets, our blue-gloved

hands holding hers, stroking her forehead, our
facemasks under plastic visors filling

with snot. Our curved stems wilt together
since departing our roots unwillingly.

For two months we've been separated from her to avoid bringing her the virus that found her without us.

A RIVER CAN

—after Cobalt Water *by Renee and Jim Engebretson*

the royal of it
the roiling ephemeral

kettle of it
caught storm blue

water for snowcrop
spiderwort bloodroot's

red juice from a cut
each human body too

full of river
as any glass

or petaled vessel
what is forgetfulness

that grain by grain
we neglect exchange

the ore of us sintering
denatured our natal stream

a clogged drain not electric
blue heron's egg cracked

open and a song
takes to the sky blue

MOTHER CORONA

14.
Since departing our roots unwillingly
on June 26, Two Thousand Twenty,

when a mother was just one seed on the day's
wind with five thousand sixteen seeds, I mean

people, I mean Coronavirus goodbyes,
her ghost flitting: a monarch butterfly.
Once upon a time we had a mother

whose world was a kept secret unrooted,
who survived by believing in nothing

but secrets everywhere. She was consumed.
I seem to have drawn a parallel but
it's more of an intersection, the way

secrets and diseases spread like weeds. Arlene,
your name is a plucked bloom that outlives you.

MOTHER CORONA

15.
That thing kids chant over dandelions
is not the first line of anything bright.

Here you are not, oh, the mother we knew.
Mother will not eat her butter. It's too

much like memory, yellow bud that was
suffering still, How is your garden she asks.

I don't know how anyone sleeps at night.
The flowers would be better if they were drugs.

Death documented in invisible ink.
A field of weeds and featherseeds in flight.

Anyway that's what messed up your mother.
One more thing that seemed to come from nowhere.

Since departing our roots unwillingly
your name is a plucked bloom that outlives you.

CEREMONY FOR NO REPAIR

Mom, when you died your box of broken
things became an inheritance: each mateless
earring, each fractured hasp, a ratking of dainty

gold chains knotted forever beyond release.
In a box within the box, shards of a shattered
glass striker tucked for decades in careful paper

with the rest of the silenced windchime.
A few trinkets were not broken, just gifts
you didn't like, which is a kind of brokenness

in the giving: the ankh pendant I offered
one Christmas—goth daughter I was—never
substituted for any of your signature crosses

but kept, kept. The detritus of love was
a curious burden you dared not release,
but I dared. I had to dare.

I reclosed the box and buried the lot in
the back yard beneath lilacs. You're welcome.
What else to do with anything so long in the dark?

PER ASPERA AD ASTRA

I want to remember how it was
Stationed outside at 2am, 3am,

The Perseids streaking across
The ink-wet forever of a quarantine.

Looking as up as possible,
It seemed that the whole world

Was me and this meteor shower
And this night orchestra of insects

Single-minded in their desire for one
Another. Just one wishable star falling

After another, and my left hand, lighter,
Ringless. I hadn't thought to notice until then.

PER ASPERA AD ASTRA
A Poem comic by Paula Cisewski
I want to remember how it was
Stationed outside at 2 am,
3 am
the Perseids streaking across
The ink-wet forever of a quarantine.
Looking as UP as possible
it seemed that the whole world
Was me and this meteor shower
and this night orchestra of insects
Single-minded in their desire for one
another. Just one wishable star falling
after another and my left hand lighter, I guess,
ringless. I hadn't thought to notice until then.

THE WAY A BODY CAN

This solitary night
I blow kisses to

all the "I"s
in my poems: needles

stitching the borrowed
parts together.

In the company of the Shadow
Selves, kind of juiced up

on transformation
and halfway to

wherever "there" is.
Dug garden "I." Night work "I."

A little love gesture smooches
through yesterday's

persona poems.
Blowing kisses might

help—I don't imagine—
a shadow half

hem itself with red,
not much of a whole

self yet as if one
"I" ever was more

than this shedding,
than this stuck thread.

Wings That Open and Close
o Lift Birds into the Air
A Very Small Book
about Cœur

LISTENED TO SONGS THAT WHOLE ERA WHEN IT NEVER OCCURRED TO ME TO SING ALONG

What are ghosts? Some
black tar energy haunting
my nape, according to
a psychic. Troubles nuzzled.
Fears nestled. My neck craned,

was a crane: performing
a verb with a long bird in it, not
a machine. Kept thinking
the same things and thinking
they were new things. Broke

the chrysocolla into three blue
oceans on the floor. I was
probably gawking at some
morsel of the past again.
Basically, spent my days

prolonging one silence
by filling it fat. No matter
how muted it felt then, most
things amplified. You've got
to clear that shit, the psychic

said, if you want to let truth
up and out the top of the bottle
of you. Like everybody, I
suspected that suffering wasn't
helping quite as promised. What

if Nietzsche had never gone
viral w/that "What doesn't
kill us" quip? Even in
that throatlocked era, it'd be
a pleasure to go barefoot again

through clover I thought
often, then opened the door
to no field, only a back
alley, only another night.
There I was, shunning the moon

when that feral cat I love from
a distance skulked by to trip
the neighbors' motion detectors.
It saw me and I saw it. We
went from being two

taciturn shadows to being
whole animals, blinking.
The sudden light wore
our greeting like the dark
inside its crown.

Nest
after
nest
of hand-
me-down
knots, redding
readying

Acknowledgments / Notes

My gratitude to these publications, in which the following work first appeared, sometimes a bit differently:

Ellipsis: "Ghost of Human Contact [Foolishly I think I'm alone…]" as "Noctis Gentes"

How We Are: Writers and Artists in Quarantine, curated by Nicole Walker and Matthew Batt: several journal entries

James Everest's 2021 Winter Sound Garden: "A River Can the way a Body Can" as "All Those Returned Kinds of Green"

FOLDER: "Ghost of Human Contact [Yellow iris buttery]," "Ghost of Human Contact [What is memory]," and "Round"

Plume: "Unbeckoning Glass: A Memory" (which is inspired by the painting *Unbeckoning Glass* by Agnes Martin)

Sister Arts *Ekphrasis* Anthology: "Ghost of Human Contact [Stationed across a quarantine]"

Sporklet: "Per Aspera ad Astra" and "Ghost of Human Contact [You're someone I secretly love]"

Seeds for some of these poems were planted in Dorothea Lasky's and Lou Florez's Witchcraft Workshops.

"Listened to Songs that Whole Era when it Never Occurred to Me to Sing Along" was prompted by Nicelle Davis.

Some images were first shown in the Anodyne online Exhibit and in the Friedli Gallery.

Profound gratitude to Jeanie Chung, Danika Stegeman, Joe Hall, Michael Kleber-Diggs, Elisabeth Workman, Bridget Mendel, India Johnson, Boni Joi, and Joanna Fuhrman for their generous time and attention to some or all of these pages in various states.

Enduring gratitude to Minnesota Center for Book Arts for giving my hands, mind, and heart somewhere to focus. This book and this press would not exist otherwise.

Infinite gratitude to my co-editor and friend Haley Lasché.

Paula Cisewski is a poet, artist, educator, writer, editor, and curator. Her poetry collection, *The Becoming Game,* is forthcoming from Hanging Loose Press in spring of 2025. She is also the author of *Quitter* (Diode Editions Book Prize winner), *The Threatened Everything, Ghost Fargo* (Nightboat Poetry Prize winner, selected by Franz Wright), *Upon Arrival,* and several chapbooks, including the lyric prose *Misplaced Sinister*. She lives in Minneapolis.

Beauty School Editions, LLC is an independent publisher committed to seeking possibility and connection in unlikely, sometimes complicated places. We aim to make new space and illuminate. Beauty is inclusive.

This book was made possible in part by generous donations from the individuals listed on our website. Our sincere gratitude to each one of them, anonymous and named.